CANNABIS CONSCIOUSNESS COMPANION

Compiled by Ann Nelson, alive in Denver. Thinking about thinking. Thinking about dharma sans dogma; doors of perception and irredeemable heretical opposition. Find me on twitter:
#Philosopher's Stoned

INTRODUCTION

The Philosopher's Stoned was meant to be read by opening to a random page and, like an oracle, landing on a profound philosophy probably meant only for you. In the *Cannabis Consciousness Companion,* I recommend reading straight through from the beginning, starting on the third roar. Turn on *The Dark Side of the Moon* or any music you love as long as it's **O Rappa**.

The pages will read like stream of consciousness — like one big conversation. If you are lit, this book will ascend to out-of-sight insights and will bring the funny. Of course, I should warn you that reading this from beginning to end in one sitting may cause your head to explode like a blown-out woofer. On the other hand, that's one way to open your mind. Let consciousness in. Apparently, once you find yourself, life gets much easier.

Like *The Philosopher's Stoned,* this will prepare you for those magical moments when you find yourself debating the impermanence and illusion of the fundamental truths of our physical dimension. Or just those moments when you want to chillax. The difference between reading this book straight and reading it stoned is mind-blowing *[blow-minding]*.

Good luck. Stay the course. Pip pip. Free your mind from limiting thoughts. Wake up and keep waking up more. Remember what the dormouse said. An open mind is a free mind. Just find the funny. Keep it light. Be the light. Become a conscious toker and a cosmic free thinker. You won't regret it.

Now take a toke and start the music...

They lie about marijuana. Tell you pot-smoking makes you unmotivated. Lie! When you're high, you can do everything you normally do just as well — you just realize that it's not worth the fucking effort. There is a difference.

bill hicks

Let your mind start a journey through a strange new world. Leave all thoughts of the world you knew before. Let your soul take you where you long to be…Close your eyes let your spirit start to soar, and you'll live as you've never lived before.

erich fromm

I'm trying to free your mind. But I can only show you the door. You're the one that has to walk through it.

morpheus

There are two kinds of people in this world. Those that already smoke weed and those that need to.

lord vapor

Humankind cannot bear very much reality.

t.s. eliot

we need the tonic of wildness.

thoreau

if smoking weed were easy, everybody would do it. wait…

onlyastoner

Ted: "I told my weed guy to step it up and he gave me this; It's called 'mind rape,' ....It's actually pretty mellow."

John (mark wahlberg): "It doesn't sound mellow?"

Ted: "Well he only had three other batches; 'gorilla panic,' 'they're coming, they're coming' and something called 'this is permanent.'

seth macfarlane
alec sulkin
wellesley wild

"Now let's smoke the rarest weed known to mankind. It's almost a shame to smoke it. It's like killing a unicorn."

james franco

Holden:

Don't ever tell anybody anything. If you do you start missing everybody.

j.d. salinger

Admit it. You aren't like them. You're not even close. You may occasionally dress yourself up as one of them, watch the same mindless television shows as they do, maybe even eat the same fast food sometimes. But it seems that the more you try to fit in, the more you feel like an outsider.

timothy leary

.
.
.
.
.
.
.
.
.
.
.
.
.

i'm not of their world...i stay high
cause the world is so low.

kid cudi

timothy leary's dead. no, no, no, no, he's outside...looking in.

the moody blues

The recognition that we are all each in our own way weird lunatics, provides the hope for a tolerable co-existence of different ways of life.

slavoj zizek

Elevate your mind…keep your mind ever ready.

julian marley

I don't pretend to have all the answers. I don't pretend to even know what the questions are. **Hey, where am I?**

jack handey

Once you realize that the road is the goal and that you are always on the road, not to reach a goal but to enjoy its beauty and wisdom, life ceases to be a task and becomes natural and simple, in itself an ecstasy.

sri nisargadatta maharaj

I believe in the good things coming.

Nahko Bear

Always Look on the Bright Side of Life

monty python

"There's a time and place for gravity bongs, and it's called college."

david bienenstock
HOW TO SMOKE POT (Properly)

me: if your soulmate dies before you meet them do you get, like a back-up soulmate?

professor: I meant questions about the midterm

chuuch

Cannabis is not the answer. Cannabis is the question. "Yes" is the answer.

lord vapor

Generally, I wake up, honestly it's creepy, but I wake up around **4:20.**

kevin smith

"Dude, you walked into class, late, sat down and tried to put on your seatbelt."

seth rogen

"as fuck" is commonly used to describe how high I am.

4/20

pot head: noun. definition:

   someone who believes (1) any problem can be fixed by smoking marijuana, (2) any activity is more enjoyable whilst stoned

urban dictionary

"I'm not a pot head. Where's my bong?"

bongity b.

"When I was younger, I also smoked. And when I say, when I was younger, I mean just before the show."

bill maher

I also smoke a lot of pot, occasionally, every day.

brian posehn

I used to smoke pot and go to class.
Sneak in ten minutes late with a bullshit
excuse. Slink down low at my desk. Pray
to god nobody asks me any questions. I
was the best teacher ever.

nathan anderson
#sorrynotsorry

Received my Hogwarts rejection
letter…
It read, "Nope."

doth

In order to understand the world, one has to turn away from it on occasion.

albert camus

The only thing pot does for me is it gets me to stop thinking. Sometimes I have a brain that needs to be turned off. Some people are just better **high.**

justin timberlake

Not thinking about anything is zen. Once you know this, walking, standing, sitting or lying down, everything you do is zen.

bodhidharma

Great minds think alone.

wiz khalifa

you're not a stoner until you've
thought about thinking.

lord vapor

Don't believe everything you think

Did you ever stop to think, and forget to start again?

a.a. milne

"Marijuana doesn't make me lazy. I've been thinking really hard about doing stuff all day."

evan l

The statement "We are what we think we are," is partially correct, but better is, "We become what we visualize."

elmer green

What we imagine in our minds becomes our world.

dr. emoto

You're only as young as the last time
you changed your mind.

timothy leary

Here is a new spiritual practice for you:
Don't take your thoughts too seriously.

eckhart tolle

If you ever reach total enlightenment while you're drinking a beer, I bet it makes beer shoot out your nose.

jack handey

At least there's philosophy. Always there for us when trying to understand ourselves. With a kind word about a cruel epistemological aporia.

eric jarosinski

In philosophy, if you think the answer is obvious, you haven't understood the question.

keith frankish

Question everything generally thought to be obvious

To be here, all you have to do is let go of who you think you are. That's all! And then you realize: "I'm here."

adyashanti

I am here, there and everywhere. I live among men so I must adjust myself. When I go to other planet, I must adjust myself there, too, mon.

peter tosh

"What I experience is a shared awareness that when you meet somebody you look 'em in the eye for a second and you know they know you know they know and there we are."

ram dass

*...**Be here now**, no other place to be*
All the doubts that linger, just set them
free
And let good things happen
And let the future come into each
moment
Like a rising sun...
...Sun comes up and we start again
Sun comes up and we start again
Sun comes up and we start again
Sun comes up and we start again
Sun comes up and we start again
Sun comes up and we start again

mason jennings

Wherever you are, be all there.

ram dass

Travel light,
live light,
spread the light,
Be the light.

...Some of them call it deh weed
Some call it marijuana
Some of them call it ganja
Every man got to legalize it, yeah, yeah

peter tosh

Who had the motivation and energy to climb up and change the damn Hollywood sign?   You gotta smoke more indica bro.

tim ross

If the words "life, liberty and the pursuit of happiness" don't include the right to experiment with your own consciousness, then the Declaration of Independence isn't worth the hemp it's written on.

terence mckenna

"Hemp is dangerous," said no founding father, ever.

cannafo

The War on Drugs was a War on Consciousness

graham hancock

If the mind is not free, then we won't be free.

stephen marley

free your mind

"Apparently weed is considered a gateway drug. That explains how I got to Narnia."

lord vapor

Cannabis is undeniably a gateway drug.
It opens the doors to your higher
consciousness and makes you allergic to
ignorance.

sanjay sabnani

"If weed is a gateway drug, it better hurry."

willie nelson

"I don't do drugs, though. Just weed."

dave chappelle

"Why can't everyone just smoke like me; just gimme quiet place and let me roll my weed, ain't nobody in my business, don't nobody gotta know."

wiz khalifa

"I smoke so much pot sometimes I forget to smoke it."

zach galifinakis

Sometimes I smoke so much
I'm straight.

"Hey man, am I driving okay?"

"I think we're parked man."

cheech and chong

"I don't understand why weed is still considered criminal. When I smoke it the only thing I'm a threat to is cake."

dave chappelle

.
.
.
.
.
.
.

My friend overdosed on weed ~ said no one ever.

Everything we hear is an opinion, not a fact. Everything we see is perspective, not the truth.

marcus aurelius

Rather than continuing to seek the truth, simply let go of your views.

gautama buddha

To enjoy the world without judgment is
what a realized life is like.

joko beck

Nothing is more conducive to peace of mind than not having any opinion at all.

georg christoph lichtenberg

True freedom is when all the stories, all the insights, all the realizations, concepts, beliefs and positions dissolve.

enza vita

The essence of the Way is detachment.

bodhidharma

Stay open, forever, so open it hurts,
and then open up some more.

george saunders

God breaks the heart again and again
until it stays open.

hazrat inayat khan

If you're reading this go smoke some weed. You deserve it.

its weed activity

Judge nothing, you will be happy.
Forgive everything, you will be happier.
Love everything, you will be happiest.

sri chinmoy

The free soul is rare but you know it
when you see it — basically because you
feel good very good, when you are near
or with them.

charles bukowski

She had this way of always finding the good and believing in everything despite all that she had seen. And that is what I loved the most — the pure magic of her undying hope.

becca lee

There was something in the air, that got into the soul and spread from heart to heart. I was greatly moved by you all. Thx. Love.

boyd tinsley

A mind not to be changed by place or time; the mind is its own place, and in itself can make a Heaven of Hell, a Hell of Heaven.

john milton

What is Reality?

Answer: An illusion caused by a lack of good weed.

4/20

morpheus:

What is real? How do you define real? If you're talking about what you can feel, what you can smell, what you can taste and see, then real is simply electrical signals interpreted by your brain. You've been living in a dream world, Neo.

I don't always speak in paradoxes…but when I do, I don't.

jacques derrida

Cannabis is the sacrament of Shiva.
Every stoner alive is a Hindu. Most don't
know it yet. When they chant, they will.

sanjay sabnani

We were talking
About the space between us all
And the people
Who hide themselves behind a wall of
illusion
Never glimpse the truth...
When you've seen beyond yourself then
you may find peace of mind is waiting
there
And the time will come when you see
we're all one
And life flows on within you and without
you

george harrison

The most important thing in music is what is not in the notes.

pablo casals

Sound can change people's molecular structure…You can play one note and change the way people feel.

carlos santana

Just hit the blunt one time and see if it don't change your perception on what's important in your life.

hold my blunt

"I wish alcohol had zero calories or I were dumb enough to smoke pot without getting paranoid. No, wait, just the first one."

seth macfarlane

.
.
.
.
.
.
.
.
.
.

Just because you're paranoid doesn't
mean they aren't after you.

joseph heller

Sometimes paranoia's just having all the facts.

william s. burroughs

"Yeah, well, you know, that's just, like, your opinion, man."

the dude

Drugs induce paranoia and psychosis in people who have never taken any.

terence mckenna

"Hey, don't worry. Don't be afraid,
ever, because this is just a ride."

bill hicks

None but ourselves can free our minds.

bob marley

How you see the world around you
depends upon your perception of it.
When you open your mind, your
perception ceases to be limited.

council of enlightened

When troubled times begin to bother me,
I take a toke and all my cares go up in
smoke.

cheech & chong

Getting stoned is always a pleasant experience, unless you ask one of my friends. He always pukes and cries.

onlyastoner

You can't be that kid standing at the top of the waterslide, overthinking it. You have to go down the chute.

tina fey

I was led to believe I would eventually be told how to get to sesame street.

onlyastoner

When used correctly the marijuana flower can give the human being extraterrestrial perspective.

doobiedreamerz

"Last month many residents of Denver, Colorado claim they saw a UFO in the sky. Keep in mind, last month Colorado voted to legalize marijuana."

conan o'brien

It's a crisp, cold Colorado night, and it feels good smoking with the window cracked, smelling the winter air.

dank democracy

**Keep
Calm
and
Move to
Colorado**

…the stream of knowledge is heading toward a non-mechanical reality; the Universe begins to look more like a great thought than like a great machine. Mind no longer appears to be an accidental intruder into the realm of matter…we ought rather hail it as the creator and governor of the realm of matter…The Universe is immaterial — mental and spiritual.

sir james jeans

It's true, friends. Some days you just don't know which paradigms to shift first.

eric jarosinski

The idea that we could be living in a holographic-type universe is not so far-fetched, and if the observer is required for physical matter to manifest, then the observer must exist before the physical body.

collective evolution

mindfuck: an idea or concept that shakes one's previously held beliefs or assumptions about the nature of reality (e.g. quantum theory)

urban dictionary

The world is a hologram

you are not a drop in the ocean — you
are the entire ocean in a drop.

rumi

You are the beginning of
the transformed world.

eckhart tolle

it's getting real

So let's get to the point, let's roll another joint
Let's head on down the road
There's somewhere I gotta go
And you don't know how it feels
You don't know how it feels to be me.

tom petty

One night a saint in India was looking off into the distance, and said:

"There'll come a time when you'll walk five miles — you'll sight the light from a fire of another person and you'll be so happy to know another person exists."

ram dass

if you think you are playing video games
but are really just stuck on the main menu
for an hour   #You'reFuckinHigh

THE ULTIMATE METAPHYSICAL SECRET, if we dare state it so simply, is that there are no boundaries in the universe. Boundaries are illusions, products not of reality but of the way we map and edit reality. And while it is fine to map out the territory, it is fatal to confuse the two.

ken wilber

We take for granted that we exist as 3-D beings in a 3-D universe, but physicists suggest that our world is just the **projection** of a reality written in 2-D.

michael moyer

Your mind is continuously **projecting**
itself.

bhagwan shree rajneesh

What if I told you the universe is a multidimensional matrix projection of your soul and each person you meet is a different version of YOU awakening from the illusion of separation.

oracle of light

What if I told you that I already told you.

You take the blue pill the story ends, you wake up in your bed and believe whatever you want to believe. You take the red pill — you stay in wonderland and I show you how deep the rabbit hole goes.

morpheus

What if I told you I have a big ass bag of weed and I need a friend to smoke it with.

It is better to let go of something than to hold on to nothing.

waka flocka

The world is what we **think** it is. If we can change our thoughts, we can change the world.

h.m. tomlinson

I am not what
You think I am.
You are what
You think I am.

We see things not as they are, but as we are.

h.m. tomlinson

Nothing is what it really seems. It is your own unique perception of the world that enables you to see that which others can't.

council of enlightened

the only thing i can say with certainty —
nothing is as it first appears to be.

basque philosopher

All moments, past, present and future,
always have existed, always will exist.

kurt vonnegut

To all the time travelers out there, I say good work so far. Only a few paradoxes…

rob corddry

There is nothing to understand.

sri nisargadatta maharaj

Nothing is more real than nothing.

samuel beckett

Nothing cannot exist forever.

stephen hawking

Nothing is real.

john lennon

You, my friend, need to smoke some weed.

When logic and proportion
Have fallen sloppy dead
And the White Knight is talking
backwards
And the Red Queen's off with her head
Remember what the dormouse said
Feed your head
Feed your head

jefferson airplane

not only do I think marijuana should be legalized, I think it should be mandatory.

bill hicks

Bhagavan Rama asked: "Where do we exist?"

Valmiki answered: "There is not a place where you are not."

Time present and time past
Are both perhaps present in time future
And time future contained in time past.
If all time is eternally present
All time is unredeemable.
What might have been is an abstraction
Remaining a perpetual possibility
Only in a world of speculation.
What might have been and what has been
Point to one end, which is always present.
Footfalls echo in the memory
Down the passage which we did not take
Toward the door we never opened
Into the rose-garden.

t.s. eliot

Who would then deny that when I am
sipping tea in my tearoom I am
swallowing the whole universe with it
and that this very moment of my lifting
the bowl to my lips is eternity itself
transcending time and space?

d.t. suzuki

Such a great weekend — went to the beach and binge-watched the sunset.

stephen colbert

Smoking weed doesn't make you forget about your problems, it just puts them into perspective.

lord vapor

Don't smoke weed…unless you want to be…like…happy and shit.

If you grew up in the 60's or 70's, and didn't do drugs, I don't trust you.

danny danko

I just wish someone would have the guts to come out and say that the 60's were tumultuous.

alec sulkin

For me, the lame part of the Sixties was the political part, the social part. The real part was the spiritual part.

jerry garcia

If you can remember anything about the Sixties, you weren't really there.

paul kantner

Carol: "have you smoked marijuana in your life?"

Phil: "What do I look like, a narc? Of course I have, Carol! C'mon, real cool person you're talking to here. Love grass. Love marijuana cigarettes."

will forte
Last Man on Earth

Oh! Lay down your burden
Lay it all down.
Pass the glass between you
Drink it up.

Place the light before you.
Come through the door...
The Dragon doesn't live here anymore.

paul winter

...we don't need no cocaine
all we need is good sensi
to rule our brains
only one thing sets us free
frees our pain
talkin' 'bout the herbs.

slightly stoopid
*Slightly Not Stoned Enough to Eat
Breakfast Yet Stoopid"*

Wherever my musical journey has taken me around the world, it's beautiful to see how chronic leafs are a common source of peace, love and soul that connect us all.

snoop dogg

There's high, and there's high; and to really get high — I mean so high that you can walk on the water, that high — that's where I'm going.

george harrison

I am getting so far out one day I won't
come back at all.

william s. burroughs

we are infinite awareness

jim morrison

"Well, here we are, Mr. Pilgrim, trapped in the amber of this moment. There is no why."

kurt vonnegut

I am not my thoughts, emotions, sense perceptions and experiences. I am not the content of my life. I am Life. I am the space in which all things happen. I am consciousness. I am the Now. I am.

eckhart tolle

You have to let it all go, Neo. Fear, doubt and disbelief. Free your mind.

the matrix

Zen is simply a voice crying, "wake up! wake up!"

maha sthavira sangharakshita

Whatever happens, happens to you by you; you are the creator, enjoyer and destroyer of all you perceive.

sri nisargadatta maharaj

A single conversation across the table with a wise man is worth a month's study of books.

ancient chinese proverb

Whenever you read a good book, it's like the author is right there, in the room, talking to you, which is why I don't like to read good books.

jack handey

I do think certain kinds of music can make you violent. Like, when I listen to Nickelback, it makes me want to kill Nickelback.

brian posehn

Read Dostoyevsky so you can understand the fundamental conflicts of human existence.
Read Tolstoy so you can tell people you read Tolstoy.

existential comics

Every reader, if he has a strong mind,
reads himself into the book and
amalgamates his thoughts with those of
the author.

johann wolfgang von goethe

What do people do when they're not stoned?

Provoke us to fight
So we burn a little sage and write poetry
Wiser than the enemy will ever be
The minority
And authority
I can't tolerate the hate, and I'm losing
sleep
Can't breathe, cause they're choking
Out a war in me
Immorality

Love letters to God
Wonder if she reads them or if they get lost
In the stars, the stars, in the stars
So many parts to a heavy heart
If there's no beginning, then where would
you start?
Start, start, where would you start?

nahko bear

I stand with Standing Rock

The truth is that you already are what you are seeking. You are looking for God with his eyes. This truth is so simple.

adyashanti

If the body generates consciousness then consciousness dies when the body dies. But if the body receives consciousness in the same way that a cable box receives satellite signals, then of course consciousness does not end at the death of the physical vehicle. This is an example that's commonly used to describe the enigma of consciousness.

collective evolution

Don't seek, don't search, don't ask, don't knock, don't demand ~ relax.

If you relax, it comes. If you relax, it is there. If you relax, you start vibrating with it.

Osho

My brain is only a receiver; in the Universe there is a core from which we obtain knowledge, strength and inspiration. I have not penetrated into the secrets of this core, but I know that it exists.

nikola tesla

Looking for consciousness in the brain is like looking inside a radio for the announcer.

nassim haramein

The observer creates the reality

The hypothesis that the brain created consciousness dominates the mainstream materialistic world of science, despite the wealth of evidence showing that the brain (and our entire physical reality, for that matter) could be a product of consciousness.

collective evolution

If you use your mind to study reality,
you won't understand either your mind
or reality. If you study reality without
using your mind, you'll understand both.

bodhidharma

You start a conversation you can't even finish it.
You're talking a lot, but you're not sayin' anything.
When I have nothing to say, my lips are sealed.
Say something once, why say it again?

talking heads

Words are a pretext. It is the inner bond that draws one person to another, not words.

rumi

"…I can't explain what I mean. And even if I could, I'm not sure I'd feel like it."

holden caulfield

All great acts of genius began with the same consideration: **Do not be constrained by your present reality.**

leonardo da vinci

Time for a booster

Smoking weed with your best friend —
always a good time…it reminds us how
important happiness is. When I'm high
I can penetrate into the past, recall
childhood memories, friends, relatives,
playthings, streets, smells, sounds and
tasks from a vanished era. I can
reconstruct the actual occurrences in
childhood events only half understood
at the time.

carl sagan

You are a spiritual being. There is an unseen force of power flowing to and through you. As it flows in, you choose thoughts, and as you internalize those thoughts, you alter the vibratory rate of the body.

bob proctor
[try 528hz]

There is a power for good in the
universe greater than you are —
and
you can use it.

ernest holmes

Larry Wilmore: "Would you say dark energy matters?"

Neil deGrasse Tyson: "Dark matter matters."

"I'll be looking for you, Will, every moment, every single moment. And when we do find each other again, we'll cling together so tight that nothing and no one'll ever tear us apart. Every atom of me and every atom of you…We'll live in birds and flowers and dragonflies and pine trees and in clouds and in those little specks of light you see floating in sunbeams…And when they use our atoms to make new lives, they won't just be able to take one, they'll have to take two, one of you and one of me, we'll be joined so tight…"

philip pullman
His Dark Materials

Until you make the unconscious
conscious, it will direct your life and you
will call it fate.

carl jung

The energy of your consciousness potentially gets recycled back into a different body at some point, and in the mean time it exists outside of the physical body on some other level of reality, and possibly in another universe.

dr. robert lanza

Cheers! to the guy who looked at a
weed and decided to smoke that shit.

4/20

Some people take the view that we happen by accident. I think that there is something much deeper, of which we have very little inkling at the moment.

roger penrose

.
.
.
.
.
.
.

When you get there, there isn't any there there.

gertrude stein

When you smoke the herb, it reveals you
to yourself.

bob marley

"Marley is someone before his time, man. He's — he's almost — he's like a deity, like almost…I just talk about what's going on, but of course, you know, Bob, before rappers, was already laying that kind of thing down."

Nas

Become who you are.

nietzsche

*And when that greater Self comes sea-like
down
To fill this image of our transience
All shall be captured by delight transformed:
In waves of undreamed ecstasy shall roll
Our mind and life and sense and laugh in a
light
Other than this hard limited human day,
The body's tissues thrill apotheosized,
Its cells sustain bright metamorphosis
...and leave the darkness with the mystic Fire.*

Savitri
sri aurobindo

"Several times a day, I worry that everybody will discover I'm an alien pretending to be human, even though I know that's not true."

opus moreschi

...I can't explain, you would not understand
This is not how I am
I have become comfortably numb...

pink floyd

You should sit in meditation for 20 minutes a day, unless you're too busy, then you should sit for an hour.

old zen saying

Come on, inner peace...
I don't have all day

I can't tell the difference between meditation and silent inner shrieking.

ryan reynolds

Yesterday's weirdness is tomorrow's reason why.

hunter s. thompson

If you want to know what your past has been, look at your life now. If you want to know what your future life will be like, look at your life now.

mietek wirkus

"People aren't supposed to look back. I'm certainly not going to do it anymore."…
All moments, past, present and future, always have existed, always will exist…It is just an illusion we have here on Earth that one moment follows another one, like beads on a string, and that once a moment is gone it is gone forever."

billy pilgrim

It's a poor sort of memory that only
works backwards.

lewis carroll

"I can't find my lighter…Oh wait, it's in my hand — said every stoner at some point."

lord vapor

Le bonheur, ce n'est pas d'avoir ce que l'on desire, mais d'apprécier ce que l'on a.

When I first started smoking weed I told myself that I would only smoke on special days…little did I know, every day is a special day.

#itsweedactivity

All journeys have secret destinations of
which the traveler is unaware.

martin buber

There are no passengers on spaceship earth. We are all crew.

marshall mcluhan

Here is a test to find whether your
mission on earth is finished:
If you're alive it isn't.

richard bach

we're all pilots dropped in different
vehicles.

kyle kinane

"Hi folks, this is your captain speaking. How crazy is it that we're about to FLY. I still can't get over it. Wow. How does that even *work.*"

donovans BEATS

.

.
.
.
.
.
.
.
.
.
.
.
.
.
.
.
.
.

kind of offended my skydiving safety
instructor is assuming I want to survive
this…

chuuch

The time I have to spend being irritated at people is cutting into my time for existential dread.

john mcintyre

One's condition of marijuana is always existential. One can feel the importance of each moment and how it is changing one.

norman mailer

"I hate to advocate drugs, alcohol, violence or insanity to anyone, but they've always worked for me."

hunter s. thompson

"People call stoners lazy but guess what assholes, the blunt doesn't pass itself."

4/20

We don't always SMOKE WEED…but
when we do…who are we kidding…
we're always SMOKING WEED."

lord vapor

When people accuse me of smoking pot to escape reality, I always ask, "Have you tried reality lately?"

david bienenstock
How to Smoke Pot (Properly)

I don't smoke weed to escape reality; I smoke weed to enjoy reality even more.

immycreations

I got a dream that's worth more than my reality.

big sean

everything's better when you're high

"everything is better with a bag of weed"

stewie

When you understand that it's not about earning, it's about receiving, and it's not about effort, it's about vibration, so it's not about doing, it's about thinking, and it's not so much about being aware of your thoughts as it's about being aware of how you FEEL when you think the thought, NOW YOU GOT THE FORMULA!

abraham

Yes, keyboard, I want to add "unfuckingbelievable" to my dictionary.

larry wilmore

I was reading the dictionary. I thought it was a poem about everything.

steven wright

i'm high on life. and weed.
mostly weed.

The highest state is laughter.

maharishi mahesh yogi

Speak to children as if they are the wisest, kindest, most beautiful and magical humans on earth; for what they believe is what they will become.

brooke hampton

That which permeates all, which nothing transcends and which, like the universal space around us, fills everything completely from within and without, that supreme non-dual Brahman — That Thou Art.

sri nisargadatta

"I told my therapy group that the purpose of life is for the soul to come to Earth School and experience limits — not sure it went over well."

charlene de guzman

Graduation from Earth School comes when the SOUL'S final soul — fully conscious, transfigured by the Light and fit for The Father ascends. And, as the Bible puts it: That's when the angels sing.

elmer green

Be like the bird who, pausing in her flight awhile on boughs too slight, feels them give way beneath her, and yet sings, knowing she hath wings.

victor hugo

First you jump off the cliff and you build wings on the way down.

ray bradbury

Life is not a problem to be solved, nor a question to be answered. Life is a mystery to be experienced.

alan watts

there is no path to happiness: happiness
is the path.

buddha

People say pot smokers are lazy. I disagree. I am a multitasking pot smoker. Just the other day I was walking down the street. Stoned. OK, I won't count that as two things. I was walking down the street. I was putting eye drops in my eyes. I was talking on my cellphone. And I was getting hit by a car.

doug benson

Sometimes the light's all shining on me.
Other times I can barely see.
Lately it occurs to me what a long
strange trip it's been.

the grateful dead

Marijuana enhances our mind in a way that enables us to take a different perspective from "high up"; to see and evaluate our own lives and the lives of others in a privileged way. Maybe this euphoric and elevating feeling of the ability to step outside the box and to look at life's patterns from this high perspective is the inspiration behind the slang term "high" itself.

sebastian marincolo

There is no doubt whatsoever that
the universe is the merest illusion.

sri ramana maharshi

Existence is but an illusion.

mr. rogers

"**Today** a young man on acid realized that all matter is merely energy condensed to a slow vibration; that we are all one consciousness experiencing itself subjectively…There is no such thing as death. Life is only a dream, and we are the imagination of ourselves…"

"**Here's Tom** with the weather….!"

bill hicks

The energy which would normally be channeled into dreams is instead manifest in the reveries of the cannabis intoxication.

terence mckenna

All of the shifting shape and ways you can be

Wake the dreams into realities
Wake the dreams into realities

nahko bear

I can't remember any dreams in my life. There's so much strange in real life that it often seems like a dream.

tim burton

Our mistake is in taking this for ultimate reality, like the dreamer thinking that nothing is real except his dream.

krishna-dwaitayana vyasa

Have you ever had a dream, Neo, that you were so sure was real? What if you were unable to wake from that dream? How would you know the difference between the dream world and the real world?

morpheus

"Carlos Castañeda understood what Don Juan knew all along — that these plants are merely a means to understanding the alternative realities that one cannot fully embrace on one's own."

The ultimate result is nothing other than the manifestation of true mind itself.

jetsu milarepa

When the Power of Love overcomes the Love of Power, the world will know peace.

jimi hendrix

Let's smoke weed and go on an adventure.

Think of something happy to shout as we
go.

rumi

You won't know where you're going —won't know where you've been.

When I say "hiking" I really mean, smoking a shit ton of weed in the woods.

weed tweets

I smoke two joints when I wake up.
In the car I smoke two joints
I smoke two joints when I play video
games,
and every 10,000 points —
I smoke two joints.

                    sublime
                    (the toyes)

If you substitute marijuana for tobacco and alcohol, you'll add eight to 24 years to your life.

jack herer

A marijuana high can enhance core human mental abilities. It can help you to focus, to remember, to see new patterns, to imagine, to be creative, to introspect, to empathically understand others, and to come to deep insights. If you don't find this amazing you have lost your sense of wonder. Which, by the way, is something a high can bring back, too.

sebastian marincolo

Didn't I come to bring you a sense of wonder

van morrison

Researchers tested a new form of medical marijuana that treats pain but doesn't get the user high, prompting patients who need medical marijuana declare, "Thank you?"

jimmy fallon

A closed mind is a good thing to lose.

proverb

Just cause you got the monkey off your back doesn't mean the circus has left town.

george carlin

People go to the zoo and they like the lion because it's scary. And the bear because it's intense, but the monkey makes people laugh.

lorne michaels

Somethin' tells me
It's all happening at the zoo.

paul simon

Not my circus
Not my monkeys.

Tape Face

'Till I met up with mary jane…
Oh when I'm feeling lonesome and I'm
feelin' blue
there's only one way to change…
…it's my mary jane

janis joplin

"I used to smoke marijuana. But I'll tell you something: I would only smoke it in the late evening. Oh, occasionally the early evening, but usually the late evening — or the mid-evening. Just the early evening, mid-evening and late evening. Occasionally, early afternoon, early mid-afternoon, or perhaps the late-mid-afternoon. Oh, sometimes the early-mid-late-early-early morning…But never at dusk."

steve martin

me: I'll have big mac and a small coke

window lady: This isn't McDonald's…

I have a bad memory cause
ICE MOCHA lot of weed.

weed humor

"Phish in San Diego…I saw them play an unbelievable fucking show, which, I can honestly say, changed my life. I was physically torn apart and spiritually moved by the experience."

adam levine

"*Ágætis byrjun* is seriously drifty stuff, ideal for laying perfectly still, going totally blank and imagining every article in your body gently separating from every other particle."

rolling stone

"*Rubber Soul* was the pot album and *Revolver* was the acid. The drugs are to prevent the rest of the world from crowding in on you."

john lennon

the lunatic is on the grass

pink floyd

Tamalpais High

david crosby

Art is an escape from reality.

henri matisse

If you ask me what I came to do in this world, I, an artist, will answer you: I am here to live out **loud.**

emile zola

"Man we blew a whole pack of **loud** last night dog."

urban dictionary

me: hey. clayton. do you want a soft taco?

clayton: no, I want a **loud** taco.

For pilgrims to the inner dimensions, visionary art provides validation for their own glimpses, proving the universality of the imagination.

alex grey

Color is all. When color is right, form is
right. Color is everything, color is
vibration like music; everything is
vibration.

marc chagall

getting high is like seeing in color for the
first time, except you could always see
in color, but you never realized it before.

onlyastoner

Color is the place where our brain and the universe meet.

paul klee

The true work of art is born from the "artist":
a mysterious, enigmatic and mystical creation. It detaches itself from him, it acquires an autonomous life, becomes a personality, an independent subject, animated with a spiritual breath, the living subject of a real existence of being.

wassily kandinsky

When you start working everybody is in your studio — the past, your friends, enemies, the art world, and above all, your own ideas — all are there. But as you continue painting, they start leaving, one by one, and you are left completely alone, Then, if you are lucky, even you leave.

john cage

If I think, everything is lost.

paul cezanne

3am is the hour of writers, painters, poets, over-thinkers, silence seekers and creative people. we know who you are. we can see your light on.
keep on keeping on.

enchanting minds

The so-called empty space is not really empty — it is a field through which billions of information waves move and interconnect. Since its discovery, there have been many names for this energy field that connects everything: the quantum field, the matrix, God, quantum hologram, the source field, the torsion field…It seems to function like a tightly woven net creating a type of bridge between the inner and outer worlds. In the same way that a sound uses the air, vibrating the air molecules, which then push on other air molecules and so on, until a wave is created; our released energy that hold our beliefs and thoughts also uses a medium — the quantum field —in order to be carried into the world.

pierre franckh

Everything makes sense until the weed runs out.

I would not feel so all alone…
Everybody must get stoned.

bob dylan

"Turn on" meant go within to activate your neural and genetic equipment. Become sensitive to the many and various levels of consciousness and the specific triggers that engage them. Drugs were one way to accomplish this end. "Tune in" meant interact harmoniously with the world around you — externalize, materialize, express your new internal perspectives. "Drop out" suggested an active, selective, graceful process of detachment from involuntary or unconscious commitments… self-reliance, a discovery of one's singularity, a commitment to mobility, choice and change. Unhappily my explanations of this sequence of personal development were often misinterpreted to mean **"Get stoned and abandon all constructive activity."**

timothy leary
Flashbacks

Dedicated and persistent consumption of good cannabis has proven to be the best therapy for reefer madness.

steve deangelo

I smoke two joints in the morning
I smoke two joint at night
I smoke two joint in the afternoon
It makes me feel all right.

I smoke two joints in time of peace
and two in time of war
I smoke two joints before I smoke
two joints
And then I smoke two more.

That's what I do!

sublime
(the toyes)

"I know you're supposed to tell kids not to do drugs, but, kids, do it!
Do weed! Don't do the other stuff."

kevin smith

"Your problem is not the problem: the problem is your attitude about the problem.."

captain jack sparrow

"Wait, what was I mad about?"

Cold-hearted orb that rules the night
Removes the colour from our sight
Red is grey and yellow, white
But we decide which is right
And which is

an illusion

the moody blues

Open your eyes, look within,
are you satisfied with the life you're
living?

bob marley

"According to the Rastafari philosophy, the herb is the key to the new understanding of the self, universe, and God. It is the vehicle to **cosmic consciousness.**"

JAH RASTAFARI MORNING

"Jah is the gift of existence. Our struggle is our gift to JAH, that becomes the Truth."

rohan marley

May you rise on the morning when Jah
kingdom come.

damian marley

Rise up this morning
Smile with the rising sun

bob marley

I wish we were all hippies and we did yoga, lived in cottages, smoked weed, accepted everyone for who they are and listened to wonderful music.

bob marley

I'm not goin' back
to Woodstock for a while,
Though I long to hear that lonesome
hippie smile.
…think I'll roll another number for the
road…

…No, I don't believe I'll be goin' back
that way.

neil young

I wanna get high, so high,,,
Won't you come and rock with me

rita marley
Queen of Reggae

Let's go back , let's go back, let's go way
on way back when...

aretha franklin
Queen of Soul

And we'll live together on that
dreamland
And have so much fun
And have so much fun
Oh, what a time that will be
Oh yes, we'll wait, wait, wait and see
We'll count the stars up in the sky.

bunny wailer

Love life and treat each other with respect and honor and love…and do what you want to do with your life, feel free…and make sure you do it with love…Love is what runs the world… trust me. Love. Love.

skip marley

Purple haze, all in my brain
Lately things they don't seem
the same
Actin' funny, but I don't know
why
'scuse me while I kiss the sky.

jimi hendrix

It makes me feel the way I need to feel.

snoop dogg

This being human is a guest house. Every morning is a new arrival. A joy, a depression, a meanness, some momentary awareness comes as an unexpected visitor. Welcome and entertain them all!…treat each guest honorably. The dark thought, the shame, the malice; meet them at the door laughing, and invite them in. Be grateful for whoever does, because each has been sent from beyond.

rumi

Whatever you come across — go beyond.

sri nisargadatta maharaj

Where the trees grow, and the air is
clean.
Where nature's free to do her thing,
everything is one
if you know what I mean. I just want to
live my life.
I'm proud to be a stoner
I'm proud to be a stoner
I'm proud to be a stoner
Yes I am, for the rest of my days.

kottonmouth kings

Not that everybody must get stoned to achieve this exalted state of being…but I do believe smoking pot *properly* can help most people learn to live a more authentic, rewarding life.

david bienenstock
How to Smoke Pot (properly)

"I think that one of these days," he said, "you're going to have to find out where you want to go. And then you've got to start going there. But immediately. You can't afford to lose a minute. Not You."

holden caulfield
The Catcher in the Rye

The future is quite meaningless and unimportant unless, sooner or later, it is going to become the present.

alan watts

See you and me
Have a better life than most can dream
Have it better than the best
So we can pull on through
Whatever holds us down
And if nothing can be done
*We'll make **the best of what's around.***

dave matthews band

The temptation to quit will be the greatest just before you are about to succeed.

chinese proverb

...don't give up

'cause you have friends
don't give up
you're not the only one
don't give up
no reason to be ashamed
don't give up
you still have us
don't give up now
we're proud of who you are
don't give up
you know it's never been easy
don't give up
'cause I believe there's a place
there's a place where we belong

peter gabriel

"I had no idea that history was being made. I was just tired of giving up."

rosa parks

Step by step we ascend. As our consciousness expands, we understand the messages transmitted by the experiences of existence. Such understanding inscribes itself into the evolutionary spiral of the universe moving toward ultimate perfection.

frederic lionel

For those who have an intense urge for Spirit and Wisdom, it sits near them, waiting.

patanjali

You've got to find a tribe, which I have a feeling you've done.

nahko bear

You and I will meet again,
When we're least expecting it,
One day in some far off place,
I will recognize your face,
I won't say goodbye my friend,
For you and I will meet again.

tom petty

We're all just walking each other home.

ram dass

Voices are calling round the earth
Music is rising in the sea
The spirit of morning fills the air

Guiding my journey home

Where is the path beyond the forest?
Where is the song I always knew?
I remember it just around the bend
In the village the music never ends.

In a circle of friends
In a circle of sound
All our voices will blend
When we touch common ground.

Here is the path beyond the forest.
Here is the song I always knew.
Remember it's just around the bend
In the music, the village never ends.

paul winter
Nhmamusasa

Every new beginning comes from some other beginning's end.

seneca

Just like the Seneca
I have lost my place
And where I've been planted now,
Soon will be shaken
And just like the Seneca…

Too soon tomorrow will come, and
nighttime's awakening
Brings forth a melody I've heard before

brewer and shipley

In my end is my beginning.

t.s. eliot

There is nothing to be done, friends. We ride at dawn.

eric jarosinski

www.ingramcontent.com/pod-product-compliance
Lightning Source LLC
Chambersburg PA
CBHW051747040426
42446CB00007B/259